ANTHONY THWAITE

A PORTION FOR FOXES

OXFORD   LONDON   NEW YORK
OXFORD UNIVERSITY PRESS
1977

Oxford University Press, Walton Street, Oxford OX2 6DP

OXFORD LONDON GLASGOW NEW YORK
TORONTO MELBOURNE WELLINGTON CAPE TOWN
IBADAN NAIROBI DAR ES SALAAM LUSAKA ADDIS ABABA
KUALA LUMPUR SINGAPORE JAKARTA HONG KONG TOKYO
DELHI BOMBAY CALCUTTA MADRAS KARACHI

ISBN 0 19 211872 2

*Printed in Great Britain by
The Bowering Press Ltd
Plymouth*

for
Ronald and Marie Ewart

ACKNOWLEDGMENTS

SOME of these poems were first published in *Antaeus, Encounter, The Listener, London Magazine, New Poems 1973–1974, New Poems 1975, New Poems 1976, New Poetry 1* and *2, New Review, Phoenix, Poetry Book Society Christmas Supplements 1974* and *1975, Poetry Dimension 1* and *3, Time Was Away: The World of Louis MacNeice, Times Literary Supplement, Young Winter's Tales 7.* 'Jack' first appeared as a Cellar Press pamphlet, and 'By the Sluice' and 'Mr Warrener' as Mandeville Press Dragoncards. 'A Girdle Round the Earth' was the result of a commission by the Globe Playhouse Trust, and appeared in *Poems for Shakespeare 5.* 'A Portion for Foxes' was first used as part of the Greater London Arts Association's 'Dial a Poem' scheme. Several were broadcast by the BBC.

CONTENTS

The Unnamable   1
The Procession   2
By the Sluice   3
Metamorphosis   4
The Simple Life   5
Boundaries   6
Hearing Japanese Again   7
Sailing to Failaka   8
At the Indus   9
Sarajevo   10
A Moment in the South   11
At the Ironmonger's   12
Stereoscope: 1870   13
To the Veteres   14
Rescue Dig   15
Digging a Saxon Cemetery   16
Witch Bottles   17
By the City Wall   18
At Ely   19
Eccles   20
Thomas   21
A Portion for Foxes   22
Marriages   23
Spool   24
Two Poems from the Urdu   25
Vignette and Text   25
'Life and other contingencies'   26
'Tell it slant'   27
Simple Poem   28
Essays in Criticism   29
On Consulting 'Contemporary Poets of the English
     Language'   30
A Girdle Round the Earth   33
My Oxford   35
Remembering a Poet   37
For Louis MacNeice   38

Heptonstall: New Cemetery   40
Mr Warrener   42
At the Shrine of Santa Zita   43
Jack   44
On the Mountain   45
Waking   46
Called For   47

THE UNNAMABLE

It creeps away to die, like animals,
But does not die. It burrows in the thick
Compost at ends of gardens, fetches up
Pecking at attic skylights, with the lock
Turned tight with rust, unable to escape.
It frets and rustles, uttering frail calls.

Nothing can heal or help it. Seek it out,
It will go deeper, further. It won't want
Your rescue or your comfort, knowing best
What finds may ferret out, what cures may kill.
You recognise the sounds, you smell the scent:
More, you too crouch in darkness, where an animal
Crawls on all fours, head down, the collapsing tunnel.

THE PROCESSION

And when you have waited there so patiently
And at last the great procession passes by
With those sad, slow tunes you hummed interminably,
How will you join them? Will you somehow try
To draw attention with a slogan scratched
Hurriedly on a bit of paper, sound
A trumpet from the window where you watched,
Hope that by standing by you will be found
Among the million others? None of these.
No matter how confused and large the crowd,
Or how well-disciplined and separate
Those solemn marchers, you will step with ease
Down from the jostling pavement, be allowed
To join them. And you will not hesitate.

BY THE SLUICE

It pulses like a skin, at dusk
Is shaken like dusty silk. The current moves
But takes its impetus and gathers speed
Only beyond the sluice-gate. Here, the faint
Shudders, the morse of water almost trapped,
Perform half mesmerised, half dying too.

Yet are not dying: those trembling dots, those small
Reverberations, rise from what is hidden—
Scatters of minnows, nervous hair-triggered fry—
Grasping at sustenance, grabbing at what is given,
Submerged ferocities, brute delicacies.

What have I hidden here, or let go, lost,
With less to come than's gone, and so much gone?
Under the gate the river slams its door.

METAMORPHOSIS

Something is changing.
                       Soft fold on fold of flesh
Loosen, go liquid, swell, are filled with sighing.
The moistened petals melt into a cud,
Are eaten and renewed, let down their rain
Somewhere above, are salt as sea or blood.
The wound opens, closes, aches again.

The body's instruments, the choir of love,
Tremble and falter; stumbling, become one,
Singing of such an ecstasy as can move
Habitual gestures or inert repose
Into the dance of animals, the groan
Dashed from the dropping petals of a rose
As thorns thrust stiffly in a summer wind,
And pulse and impulse, leaping, fall behind.

THE SIMPLE LIFE

The simple life is breathing limitless air
In a broad countryside where minor roads
Curve behind hedges, vanish among fields.
Work there is lopping firewood, building fires
That have no use but ornamenting rooms
Large, white and objectless, reflecting light
Cast through clear windows from a temperate stream.
All things are reconciled, the past is calm.

There are times when one lives it, hours or days like this,
Steady and still, not as imagined when
The future seemed a wilder, fiercer land,
Potholed with mysteries, littered with fallen loot
Abandoned by forerunners whose great tombs
Lay in a landscape gaunt as Gordale Scar,
Where difficulty tasted danger's blood
And what was simple lay long miles ahead.

BOUNDARIES

A stream, a fence, a hedge, another fence,
A ditch, a bank, and then the river's width :
Boundaries, margins ruled with nonchalance
Or so it seems now, when the length and breadth
Of lands measured in furlongs, perches, poles
Are no more than forgotten schoolroom stuff.
Across patched fields a six-lane highway rolls
Heedless of usufruct and tithes. Enough
To call it all by letter, number, say
It runs from A to B and gets you there
More quickly than four roads did yesterday.
Yet borders and old boundaries lie where
Highways avoid a ditch, a stream, some way
Where men once paced out land with jealous care,
Knowing each fence and hedge as if Domesday.

HEARING JAPANESE AGAIN

Liquid, glottal, with other sounds
Caught in the throat and gargled,
This speech avoids
The firm, peremptory plosives I know best.
The withdrawn hiss of concurrence or deference
Hovers over long-vowelled nods and becks,
The pause-words of politeness.

Raised to hieratic pitch, it comes through masks
Enunciating ghosts and demons,
Or with a plaintive monotonous whine
Is thought proper for children on the stage.
But this is conscious artifice—
The demotic is strange enough, heaven knows,
Heard in the street or floating into the garden.

Hearing it now again, after fifteen years,
The apartness of it chills and startles me
Like no other familiar but unlearnt tongue :
It is as if the air
Were full of the growl of feudal princeling doves
Making obeisance to a hawk that hovers
Above them, its beak impatient to stop the parleying.

SAILING TO FAILAKA

With a slap, a heave, a steadying rush, the launch
Smacked into waves, swerved into spray,
Roaring across the bay
Through mirage, rainbow, sun's incessant drench.

On the other side, ruins, huts, goats, sand, all
Components of simplicity together
In the clear weather,
True isolation, desert pastoral.

A slice of the primitive life quite out of touch
With what was, for seven hours, left behind
And out of mind.
No, the whole expedition wasn't much,

A way of avoiding the Cadillac's arrogant summons
For something rather less than half a day :
Though out across the bay
I see it as clearly now as I saw it once—

The imagined fallen limestone, cairns among thorns
Where the goats feed, and a single wind-pump blows
Where a bent palm grows,
While here the night is impatient with radios, car-horns.

Lost places longed for, paradises lost :
A stone inscribed in Greek by some explorer
Who spoke to Alexander
Of this green island in a blue gulf, tossed

By spray from waves crashing from shore to shore,
Standing aloof and silent, distantly,
That place where we
Make our one brilliant landfall, then no more.

AT THE INDUS

It was wide, true, but no wider than the straits:
Most of it boulders and pebbles, the water itself
An uneven grey-blue snake, writhing in bursts
Here and there, but elsewhere sluggish with puddles.
It was not the size of that river, or the distance they'd come,
Or the men dead with delirium, or those killed in battle,
Or the exhaustion of a long campaign. But was it
Fear of the mountains rising red from the plain,
Fear of the unknown tribes on the other side?

                                        No,
However the legends go, or the histories patch it together,
The place was not ready. Over the other side,
Whatever travellers had come in their ones and twos
Over the centuries, was a possible paradise,
Untouched, immaculate, the dreamt-of place
(Though not for those who lived there: it never is).
We hesitate at those portals, whether Greek or Jew,
Bond or free, freethinker or devout, and are quiet
When, for a moment, history comes to a stop.
The regimental commanders muttered together; the battalions
                                        rested;
The leader was informed.
The bend of the river waited, and went on waiting.
The mountains, the buzzards, the plain, and the other side
Waited. The signal was given.

Then they turned back.

SARAJEVO

The name is history.
                    The thick Miljacka flows
Under its bridges through a canyon's breadth,
Fretted with minarets and plump with domes,
Cupped in its mountains, caught on a drawn breath.

There on the pavement, absurd souvenir
Of past dramatics, Princip's spoor is set:
The exact spot, the precise grid of war,
A kerbside view of a choked and bloody street

Where, regiments in step, a world moves
Or drifts away from its moorings like a ship
Propelled down-river between crowded wharfs
And only a collision can make it stop.

The muezzin calls, the bells and pigeons float
Above Sephardic, Muslim, Catholic graves:
Provincial, dated, their low stones map out
Haphazardly the place that history chose.

A MOMENT IN THE SOUTH

How different the day when the great composer
Arrived with carriages in the white piazza,
Advanced through avenues of oleander
To where his willing host, full-bearded patron
Of ancient lineage, greeted him on the loggia.

This was the place (the genius knew at once)
Where he would set that awkward second act :
A hanging garden under which the gulf
Spanned sun and haze in a long breadth of blue.
Such was his exclamation to the Count.

The tourists' brochure throbs with reverence
At this munificent and thrilling scene,
Enacted among fragrant southern trees,
When in the white piazza old men sat
Watching the dust rise from those carriages.

AT THE IRONMONGER'S

To: Messrs Trew, 12 sets no. 2 Domes of Silence, 8p per set . . .

Cabinet-hinges, casement-fasteners,
Mirror-clips and drugget-pins,
Ball-catches and bale-latches,
Curtain-hooks and curtain-rings,
Brass cabin hooks and brass escutcheons,
Cotter-keys and trammel-wedges
And, in the bottom drawer,
The domes of silence.

Coffin, casket, mausoleum,
Headstone, crucifix, monumental
Lettering etched in Latin, Hebrew,
R.I.P., Kyrie Eleison,
Sword of faith and star of David,
Ritual pyre and epicedium
And, in the bottom drawer,
The domes of silence.

STEREOSCOPE: 1870

A trick of cinematic archaeology,
A wooden toy to gaze in, among views
Where rigidly the poses now amuse
A casual audience that gasps to see
How three-dimensional such people were,
With different clothes and different hair, but all
Clear in their different rooms as we are. Tall
Men lean on mantelpieces; children stir,
Or seem to stir, restless at nursery tea;
A wife works at her crochet in a chair:
And all live in a world at which we stare
Because we recognise perspective, see
How everything is close or distant, not
Smoothed to the level pages of a book.
It is at that we almost dread to look,
Such depths, such closeness, rooted to the spot.
Peer through these eyepieces: the past goes round
Like mill-sails turning where no breezes blow,
And where we were a hundred years ago
Tugs us as something lost, not to be found,

Or sought elsewhere a hundred years from now.

TO THE VETERES

'Increasingly our attention is being drawn
To carvings set up to the Veteres.
(We give the word thus, though singular occurs
As much as plural: masculine and feminine
Forms have been found indifferently.
The spelling, too, varies enormously.)
We take it these mysterious deities
May be equated with the equally
Mysterious triads known by Dr Ross
As *genii cucullati*, "the cloaked gods",
Whose distribution also runs across
The northern frontier'.

                    My attention nods
Over the pamphlet and the photographs
Of rough-hewn altars, each one posed and lit
As if some cack-thumbed Michelangelo,
Possessed—though self-taught and illiterate—
By things outside himself, should this way show
His genius to a universe that laughs
At transcendental posturings like this.
'To the Gods, the Veteres . . .'

                    Under my eyes
Carved word and image flow together, merge,
Spreading across the scholar's cautious prose
To reach the dark rim of the very edge
That lies beyond the window's frontier:
Where Paul in Athens stooped to read the words
Inscribed upon the superstitious stone,
'To the Unknown God', and felt a moment's fear,
Possessed neither by Christ's words nor his own.

RESCUE DIG

In a fading light, working towards evening,
Knowing next day the contractors will be there,
Impatient earth-movers, time-is-money men,
And the trench, hastily dug, already crumbling
(No leisure for revetments), you're suddenly aware
Of some recalcitrant thing, as when your pen
Stubs at the page
And slips stubbornly, tripped by a grease-spot, dry
Shadow-writing. The trowel hits the edge,
Solid against solid, perhaps pottery,
Perhaps bone, something curved and flush
With earth that holds it smooth as yolk in white
And both within their shell. Feel round it, go
Teasing its edges out, not in a rush
Of treasure-hunting randomness, but quite
Firmly yet tactfully, with a patient slow
Deliberation, down
Round the bounding line that holds it, up
Its cupped outline (grey or brown?
The light is bad), letting the soil slip
Smoothly away. Too quick in your eagerness
And you'll fracture its flimsy shape, be left with scraps.
What are these folds on it? A skull's brow-ridges,
Lugs at a pot-rim? Let your hand caress
Its texture, size and mass, feel for the gaps
That may be there, the tender buried edges
Held by the earth.
Now what you want is time, more time, and light,
But both are going fast. You hold your breath
And work only by touch, nothing in sight
Except the irrelevant spots of distant stars
Poised far above your intent groping here.
Exasperated, suddenly sensing how
Absurd your concentration, your hand jars
The obstinate thing; earth falls in a damp shower;

You scrabble to save it, swearing, sweating. Now,
In the total dark,
You know it's eluded you, broken, reburied, lost,
That tomorrow the bulldozers will be back;
The thing still nameless, ageless; the chance missed.

DIGGING A SAXON CEMETERY

We approach you briskly,
Crowded clay-dwellers,
Inhabitants now well
Dispersed in your persons,
And come as callers
On hands and knees
With trowels and rulers.

You would be puzzled
To see us, scavengers
Dressed in our casual
Clothes without ritual,
Turning up ornament,
Weapon, cremation,
Plotting your downfall.

WITCH BOTTLES

Tiger-striped or leopard-spotted—thus
The usual label of the connoisseur :
But more like a toad's metallic mottling,
And having that granular coldness.
There is a heaviness, something of the earth.

Found in London clay, ten feet down,
Or on Thames mud in fragments, sloughed skins,
Nothing so sinister there. It's when they squat
Under some old cottage's hearth or threshold,
Revealed by the wreckers, that they chill the air.

The mask, with its hourglass mouth, runs with sand,
And in its belly rusty pins transfix
A chopped-out felt heart, musty in its faint
Stink of phosphate, mingling plucked hair and piss.
Charmless, a talisman exposed and shrunk

To this coagulated baleful mass :
Corroded brass, nail parings, thorns, the scum
Gathering and thickening, and now dispersed.
Somewhere a gaunt crone shrieked in the fire's heart,
Grey flesh annealed to stone, its smeltings here.

BY THE CITY WALL

A lumpish bastion of flint and tile
At the park's edge, or more precariously
Lodged by the multi-storey car park while
Shoppers lean small wheeled baskets gingerly
Against its chipped dismantlement, a style

Of vagrant dereliction—these remains
Pit civic pride against irrelevance
And both against survival. When it rains
A few find shelter there, taking their stance
Under a gap-toothed arch, hearing the drains

Glugging away municipal excesses.
Hoardings arise, disguise. A roundabout
Slices through rubble with a circus's
Fine disregard for angles. Squat and stout,
The gate-tower leans on steel-and-concrete stresses,

Shored up like an old elm choked with the blight.
Beyond it spreads the town it never knew,
Fanning far out beyond it, out of sight—
Uncircumscribed, unguarded—where the new
Ring road throws up its cloud-distempering light.

AT ELY

John Tiptoft, Earl of Worcester, d. 1470

Among the floating passengers below
This starry lantern, hale in effigy
Tiptoft lies by his brides, immaculate :
Serene and resurrected trinity.

Restored by art, cosmetic in his grace,
Watch him embrace the pure November chill,
Who at another time, alone, knelt down
And felt the axe descend on Tower Hill.

ECCLES

Cliffs sifting down, stiff grassblades bent,
Subdued, and shouldering off thick sand,
Boulders—compacted grout and flint—
Jut from a stranded beach, a land
Adhering thickly to the sea.
Tide-drenched, withdrawn, and drowned again,
Capsized, these buttresses still strain
Towards perpendicularity.

The place-name mimes the fallen church,
Abbreviated, shrunk to this
Truncated word, echo of speech,
A Latin ghost's thin obsequies
Carried by wind, answered by sea—
Ecclesia: the syllables
Curtailed, half heard, like tongueless bells
From empty steeples endlessly.

THOMAS

He crossed the dry ford and the rock-strewn course
Coming towards the city : Taxila.
Behind him, to the West, a slow loss
Of blood, not his, a show of open wounds
Not yet to be healed. He had come so far
Language had left him : he conversed in signs,
And heard replies in meaningless grunts, rough sounds,
Yelps and choked gutturals, as a dog that whines
Under a bully's blows.

                  How could he bring the word
To aliens like these? What wordless miracle
Could his dubiety raise and reveal?
Practical skills, the trade of strain and stress,
The palpable structure planned in wood and stone—
These were his passport. He had come so far
Commissioned and professional : the king's messengers
Insisted on his foreign competence,
His smart outlandishness. A palace, wrought
Out of daedalian magnificence . . .
He passed between the city walls, alone,
Trusting his still invisible harbinger,
And found the king.

                  The man who wanted proof
And touched those dripping hands, that leaking sore,
Laid out his stylus and his plans before
A king of men, and pitched the palace roof
High up in heaven, a mansion without walls,
Unprovable, unseen, where the rooftree falls
Down to its cloudy base, its starry floor.

A PORTION FOR FOXES
Psalm 63 : 10

One streaked across the road in front of us
At night—a big-brushed grey one, almost a wolf
I liked to think—somewhere in the Punjab,
Close to a village where no doubt it scavenged.
And then back home, in England,
To see what our cat brings in—
The heads of sparrows,
A mole's pink paws, the black and marbled innards
Torn from a rat, a moorhen's claws :
Rejected spoils, inedible souvenirs,
A portion for foxes.

But here there are few foxes, no wolves,
No vultures shuffling scraggily in treetops,
No buzzards drifting in sunlight, or jackal wailing
At the edge of the compound. Only a ginger cat,
Ferociously domestic, stalking the meadows
For small and lively prey, far from those borders
Where 'fall by the sword' is no Sunday metaphor
Echoed antiphonally down gentle arches,
Where even now the gleam on a raised blade
Brings back the unspeakable, the mounds of fallen
Lying in lanes, in ditches, torn, dismembered,
A sacrifice to the wrathful god, or gods :
A portion for foxes.

MARRIAGES

How dumb before the poleaxe they sink down,
Jostled along the slaughterer's narrow way
To where he stands and smites them one by one.

And now my feet tread that congealing floor,
Encumbered with their offal and their dung,
As each is lugged away to fetch its price.

Carnivorous gourmets, fanciers of flesh,
The connoisseurs of butcher-meat—even these
Must blanch a little at such rituals :

The carcasses of marriages of friends,
Dismemberment and rending, breaking up
Limbs, sinews, joints, then plucking out the heart.

Let no man put asunder . . . Hanging there
On glistening hooks, husbands and wives are trussed,
Silent, and broken, and made separate

By hungers never known or understood,
By agencies beyond the powers they had,
By actions pumping fear into my blood.

SPOOL

Envy and sloth, envy and sloth :
The two-pronged pincer and the shortened breath,
The sour mouthful, the finished youth.

On the empty platform, in the full sun,
The chattering accusations begin,
And begin again, and begin again.

Too late now for the Grand Tour,
Canals and villas in the blue air.
All journeys end on the way here.

Scratching such words on an envelope,
There is nothing to capture, nothing to keep,
And the words revolve on a loop of tape :

Saying envy and sloth, envy and sloth,
The two-pronged pincer and the shortened breath,
The sour mouthful, the finished youth.

TWO POEMS FROM THE URDU

Silence all round me, and dark clouds above.
And then she says, 'Who's there?' And I reply
'It's me—open this door that stands so high
Between us, and so difficult to move'.

And then long silence, then the wind's long cry.
Munir Niazi

Alone in the desert, endless distances
Remind me of my home, that's distant too:
And seeing home again will bring me to
Memories of such wastes, such distances.
Mohamed Iqbal

VIGNETTE AND TEXT

Pylon the fourteenth.
Lady of the knife, dancer upon blood.
I make for her the festival of the god Hak . . .
A broken key, a hawk, a libation bowl; crouched
In profile sits a judge.

                        Puzzling these things out,
I see white feathers fallen on the lawn,
Blown from the dovecote. A bright morning northward
Where trees ride the wind.

                        A messenger comes,
His face shrouded. From the south, the khamsin.
He gives me this torn papyrus, blurred with tears.

'LIFE AND OTHER CONTINGENCIES'*

Here is the set text—neat tabulations,
The bracketed asides of algebra.

Not that I understand them, but formulas exist:
The actuary tells you what they are.

At age 46, this and this are known.
Building societies have experience.

What happened earlier will recur, given
Similar circumstances. It's common sense.

Two volumes on the shelf. Now take them down:
Open at any page, at any line.

Portions of me are money. What I leave
Will prove the logic, confirm the whole design.

What cannot be accounted for is not
The text's concern. It tells you what is what.

* By P. F. Hooker, F.I.A., and L. H. Longley-Cook
M.A., F.I.A., F.C.A.S., A.S.A.
Cambridge University Press, two vols.

'TELL IT SLANT'

Precisely enigmatic. So
You draw the line : scrupulous words
Draping the naked mysteries.

Take care not to let them go.
Thoughts rise like startled birds.
Fall back on the histories.

Meticulous runes. A fearful hint
Suggested in what is not said.
Move warily among the dead.
Strike a dry spark from a flint.

Truth is partial. Name the parts
But leave the outline vague and blurred.

Mistress of passion, master of arts—
Degrees won from a cheated word.

SIMPLE POEM

I shall make it simple so you understand.
Making it simple will make it clear for me.
When you have read it, take me by the hand
As children do, loving simplicity.

This is the simple poem I have made.
Tell me you understand. But when you do
Don't ask me in return if I have said
All that I meant, or whether it is true.

I like this more than that.
That is better than this.
This means this and that.
That is what this one wrote.
This is not that at all.
This is no good at all.
Some prefer this to that
But frankly this is old hat.
That is what Thissites call
Inferior this, and yet
I hope I have shown you all
That that way lies a brick wall
Where even to say 'Yes, but . . .'
Confuses the this with the that.

Instead, we must ask 'What is this?'
Then, 'Is that *that* sort of this,
Or a modified this, or a miss
As good as a mile, or a style
Adopted by that for this
To demonstrate thisness to those
Who expect a that-inclined prose
Always from this one— a stock
Response from readers like these.'
But of course the whole thing's a trick
To make you place *them* among those
Who only follow their nose,
Who are caught on the this/that spike
But who think they know what they like.

ON CONSULTING 'CONTEMPORARY POETS OF THE ENGLISH LANGUAGE'

Dannie Abse, Douglas Dunn,
Andrew Waterman, Thom Gunn,
Peter Redgrove, Gavin Ewart,
Susan Fromberg Schaeffer, Stewart
Conn, Pete Brown, Elizabeth
Jennings, Jim Burns, George MacBeth
Vernon Scannell, Edwin Brock,
Philip Hobsbaum, Fleur Adcock,
Brian Patten, Patricia Beer,
Colin Falck, David Rokeah,
Peter Dale and David Gill,
David Holbrook, Geoffrey Hill,
David Gascoyne and John Hewitt,
William Empson and Frank Prewett,
Norman Hidden, David Wright,
Philip Larkin, Ivan White,
Stephen Spender, Tom McGrath,
dom silvester houédard,
A. Alvarez, Herbert Lomas,
D.M., R.S., Donald Thomas,
Causley, Cunningham, Wes Magee,
Silkin, Simmons, Laurie Lee,
Peter Jay, Laurence Lerner,
David Day, W. Price Turner,
Peter Porter, Seamus Deane,
Hugo Williams, Seamus Heane-
y, Jonathan Green, Nina Steane,
C. Busby Smith and F. Pratt Green,
Fullers both and Joneses all,
Donald Davie, Donald Hall,
Muldoon, Middleton, Murphy, Miller,
Tomlinson, Tonks, Turnbull, Tiller,
Barker, Brownjohn, Blackburn, Bell,
Kirkup, Kavanagh, Kendrick, Kell,
McGough, Maclean, MacSweeney, Schmidt,

Hughes (of *Crow*) and (of *Millstone Grit*),
Sir John Waller Bt. and Major Rook,
Ginsberg, Corso, Stanley Cook,
Peter Scupham, John Heath-Stubbs,
Fenton, Feinstein, both the Grubbs,
Holloway G., Holloway J.,
Anselm Hollo and Peter Way,
Logue, O'Connor, Kevin Crossley-
Holland, Hollander, Keith Bosley,
Matthew Mead and Erica Jong,
Henry Reed and Patience Strong,
Kunitz, Kizer, Kops, Mark Strand,
Creeley, Merwin, Dickey and
The other Dickeys, Eberhart,
Bunting, Wantling, Pilling, Mart-
in Booth, a Dorn and then a Knight,
A Comfort following on a Blight,
Skelton (not the Rector of Diss—
The Poet's Calling Robin, this),
Alistair Elliot, Alastair Reid,
Michael Longley, Michael Fried,
Ian Hamilton (twice—the Scot
With 'Finlay' at the end, and the other not),
Adrians Henri, Mitchell, Stokes,
Lucie-Smith and Philip Oakes,
Father Levi of the Soc-
iety of Jesus, Alan Ross,
Betjeman, Nicholson, Grigson, Walker,
Pitter, Amis, Hilary Corke, a
Decad of Smiths, a Potts and a Black,
Roberts Conquest, Mezey, Graves and Pack,
Hugh MacDiarmid (C. M. Grieve's
His real name, of course), James Reeves,
Hamburger, Stallworthy, Dickinson, Prynne,
Jeremy Hooker, Bartholomew Quinn,
Durrell, Gershon, Harwood, Mahon,
Edmond Wright, Nathaniel Tarn,
Sergeant, Snodgrass, C. K. Stead,
William Shakespeare (no, he's dead),

Cole and Mole and Lowell and Bly,
Robert Nye and Atukwei Okai,
Christopher Fry and George Mackay
Brown, Wayne Brown, John Wain, K. Raine,
Jenny Joseph, Jeni Couzyn,
D. J. Enright, J. C. Hall,
C. H. Sisson and all and all . . .
What is it, you may ask, that Thwaite's
Up to in this epic? Yeats'
Remark in the Cheshire Cheese one night
With poets so thick they blocked the light:
'No one can tell who has talent, if any.
Only one thing is certain. We are too many'.

A GIRDLE ROUND THE EARTH

'King Rear was foorish man his girls make crazy'
Says something certainly about the play.
'Prutus fall on sord for bolitical reason'
Is unambiguous, though not the way
We native-speakers might have put it, who share
A language with the undoubted global poet.
In Tokyo or Benghazi, he abides
Our questioning syllabus still, will never stay
For an answer as the candidates all stare
Into the glossaried cryptograms he hides.

O Saku Seppiya, Shakhs Bey-er, O you
Who plague the schools and universities
From Patagonia to Pakistan,
From Thailand to Taiwan, how would it please
Your universal spirit to look down
And see the turbans and burnouses bent
Above your annotated texts, or see
Simplified Tales from Lamb by slow degrees
Asphyxiate the yellow and the brown?
To pick up the quotation, 'thou art free'—

But Matthew Arnold, schools inspector, who
Saw you 'self-school'd, self-scann'd', could not have known
How distantly from Stratford and the Globe
With British Council lecturers you've flown :
Midsummer Nights in Prague and Kathmandu,
Polonius stabbed dressed in a gallabiyah,
Shylock the Palestinian refugee,
And Hamlet's father's Serbo-Croat groan,
Dunsinane transported to Peru,
Kabuki for All's Well, Noh for King Lear.

'To be or not to be. Is that a question?'
The misquotations littering the page,
The prose translations fingermarked with sweat,

You prove again, world-wide, 'not of an age
But for all time', the English Ala' ad-Din,
The Western Chikamatsu, more than both
And different from either, somehow worth
Those sun-baked hours in echoing lecture-halls,
On torn tatami or dune-drifted stage:
'Lady Macbeth is houswif full of sin',
'Prince Hel is drinkard tho of nobel berth'.

MY OXFORD

. . . memories of vomiting blindly from
small Tudor windows (Philip Larkin: *All What Jazz*)

Trinity Term . . . From somewhere down the High
A gramophone enunciates its wish
To put another nickel in, and I
Am going to have drinks with Ernle-Fyshe,
A Merton man who had a poem once
In *Time and Tide*. The future has begun.
Over by Magdalen Bridge the tethered punts
Knock at the jetty. I am having fun.

Upstairs I hand my bottle over, take
A mug of rhubarb-coloured punch, and wave
A sprightly hand at someone. 'I just make
Whatever's made from what you bring'. A grave
Critic from Keble, aged nineteen, says why
The only man is Mauriac. And then
A girl in peasant dirndl, dark and shy,
Asks me to tell her about Origen.

My bow-tie chaste, my waistcoat green brocade,
I lay the law down, and another drink.
Bells clang from colleges, her hair is swayed
By breezes at the open window. Think
How much there is to do (that villanelle,
That *Isis* piece, that essay for A4) . . .
But confidently thinking all is well
I gulp another, sinking to the floor.

Someone recites his latest poem, while
Tom Lehrer's lyrics sidle through the haze.
"What John Crowe Ransom has is purely *style*".
"Auden is only passing through a phase".

The girl has turned elsewhere. My head goes round.
Let Mauriac and co. do what they like.
I lean from the embrasure. There's the sound
Of copious liquid drenching someone's bike.

O Golden Age ! O Nineteen Fifty-Three,
When the whole world lay wide in front of me !

REMEMBERING A POET

She has no father, he no fame except
That once he knew her father. Twenty years
Of 'knew him well' for him, while what is hers
Through childhood, girlhood, womanhood was neglect
Of what made people want to know him well.
Now they are brought together to record
What they remember; but a heavy sword
Lies across every dredged-up syllable,
The friend's glib chat, the daughter's diffidence.
He is too facile, she too far away
From what she knew in a long distant day,
But both nod to the archivist's pretence
That blood and friendship have a tale to tell,
That fame's inheritance is a spool of tape
Giving a spectre an unyielding shape,
Orphan and parasite who knew him well.

FOR LOUIS MacNEICE

Your long face, like a camel's, swivels round
The long bar of the George, and stops at me
Coming in like bad news. The BBC
Recruits young graduates to rescue Sound
From all that bright-lit, show-biz sort of stuff
And I am one of them, arrived too late
For the Golden Age (the exact date
October Fifty-Seven), though enough
Remains like a penumbra of great days
To sanctify our efforts. There you stand
Aloof and quizzical, the long bar scanned
For friends or enemies, a scornful phrase
Poised to put down the parasite or bore;
But underneath that mask a lonely man
Looks out, lugubrious comedian
Or elegiac dandy, more and more
Driven into the corners of yourself.
Uncertain of your mood, after an hour
Of a shared office going slowly sour
With cigarettes and hangovers, the shelf
Above your desk capsizing with its load
Of scripts that date back sixteen years or more,
I try the Twickenham ploy, the sort of war
You relish, England–Ireland, worth an ode
Better than J. C. Squire tried long ago.
That does it. You prefer such stuff to bleak
Intensities of bookishness, and speak
With passion of who scored, and how, and know
Each quiddity of form and style and skill.
And yet I play this game only to thaw
That icy stare, because I'm still in awe
Of your most private self, that self you spill
Into the poems you keep locked away.
Looked back on now, how much I must despise
That Boswell-type with deferential eyes

Who saw you as a lion on display !
The living man eluded me. Though praise
Bitten out from those pursed, laconic lips
Astonished me, dismissal could eclipse
My universe for hours, even days.
Now that you're dead, I read you and I hear
Your nasal, almost strangled voice recite
Poems you wrote in loneliness at night,
Far from the George and parasites and beer.
My glum prosaic homage comes too late,
Ten years too late, for your embarrassment,
And yet those truant hours spent and mis-spent
Off Portland Place I humbly dedicate
To a Muse who watches, listens, is aware
Of every sell-out, every careless word,
Each compromise, each syllable that's blurred
With vanity or sloth, and whose blank stare
Chills and unmasks me as yours used to do.
Forgive me, Louis, for such well-meant verse,
Such running-on where you would have been terse,
And take the thanks I meant to give to you.

HEPTONSTALL: NEW CEMETERY

That wuthering height is not my place at all.
The graveyard on the hill at Heptonstall
Where the doomed goddess of pain was laid to rest,
Wraith of the nervous breakdown and the gas-
Oven, where the death-style is the test,
Is not my shrine. The rapt hysteric mass
Of worshippers repels my presence here,
Drawn to this spot half puzzled, half in fear.

No, I was not a man who 'knew her well',
As many did who kiss and mostly tell.
We met at parties, and in a studio
You read your poems in a hard, harsh way,
Efficiently, embodying a low
Opinion of emotional display.
You sent me small and formal notes which give
A brisk air of the bright competitive.

Did I misread you, then, misapprehend
Your downward spin when you 'embraced your end'
(The sort of euphuistic tommyrot
That floods around this grave like molten lead,
Heavy and thick and colourless and hot)?
It seems all right to say so, now you're dead,
And sounds dishonest to say otherwise
Surrounded by the acolytes and their lies.

A wilderness of syllabuses, a swamp
Of reminiscences, evasions, pomp-
osities of crass interpretation,
A hagiography of wild despair,
St Sylvia in her stance of lamentation
High on her pillar in the killing air . . .
Nothing like that rests here, nothing so brash.
The millstone turns to dust, the bones to ash.

Bells in this upland parish call to all
Who were not mourners at your funeral,
Who never toyed with different-coloured pills,
Who stayed alive through habit and through grace,
Who suffered all the usual mortal ills,
Who never read you, never saw your face
Go blank as in the mirror of your death
You breathed a legend out with your last breath.

MR WARRENER

... born in Lincoln and studied
at Lincoln School of Art, and
in London. For a time he worked
in Paris where he became a friend
of Toulouse-Lautrec, but in 1904
he returned to Lincoln to take
over the family coal merchant business.

Note in the Usher Gallery, Lincoln

Attics and absinthe, girls in shadows
Along the Seine under the gaslight,
And canvas after canvas covered
With botched-up images that hovered
In air for me to get them right
Before those placid flats and meadows
And that safe city on a hill
Beckoned me back again. And still,
Here at the roll-top desk where orders
Are neatly stacked for coke and cob,
Deliveries to Brigg or Bailgate,
The lamps all lit, and working late,
I feel my pulses leap and throb
Remembering art's old disorders.

AT THE SHRINE OF SANTA ZITA*

What are you doing here, quiet under glass,
White frills and flowered chaplet, open mouth
Hard-beaked as a tortoise?
Your leathery hands have done with knitting, baking,
Wiping and dishwashing and mending cast-offs.
You have put your feet up.

Odd at first sight that you should be presented
Thus, like a girl dressed for her confirmation,
Weary of miracles.
Yet the brown mummy spruced so smart and tidy,
Dry skin and bones made housewifely and decent,
Is a true emblem.

Seven hundred years of labour-saving gadgets
Weigh little in the balance put against you,
Gaunt patroness of habit.
It would be pleasant if such daily order,
Such steady working at routines and drudging,
Were always framed so.

Parcelling up the garbage for collection,
We catch the reek of everything neglected
Shoved into corners.
The sweeper-up we do not care to mention
Sets to his chores more ruthlessly than you did,
And sifts no rubbish.

But here you lie in your ridiculous canopy,
An old crone in a little girl's white finery,
Your left hand resting
Restlessly on the lace, as if impatient
To pick a rag up from the floor beside you
And go on dusting.

> * patron saint of domestic work, b. 1218,
> d. 1278, in S. Frediano, Lucca

JACK

She tells her grandchildren how her brother went
Off in the ambulance, his big laced boots
Heavy on the stretcher at the ends of legs
So white and thin. A family event,
The prelude to a funeral. She puts
A storyteller's shape on what she says,
And what she says holds them and makes them see
That Yorkshire street, those other, different days.

At nine years old her brother went, when we
Were nowhere, her grandchildren further off
Even than that. An accident, a death.

She pauses suddenly. The unwilled tears come,
She drops her face, and with a little cough
Stops the recital. Round the shadowy room
Children and grandchildren are silent too,
Life standing like a weight we cannot move,
Unmuscled by the thin, sharp shaft of love
That still must wound, and still the wound must show

And all that happened sixty years ago.

ON THE MOUNTAIN

The mountain meadow tilted back
Among white rocks and sprawls of berries.
We panted up the mountainside,
Plucking at clumps of grass and pausing
To catch our breath at level places.
And suddenly there, above the meadow,
Through a thin screen of trees, the sky
Exploded with a hundred swallows
Plundering the blue air's farthest reaches,
Threading and stitching side to side
Silently in the silent pasture :
A fuming swirl of wings and bodies,
Violent, disciplined, alien,
A wildness, wilderness, pure and strange.

And vanished then. The empty sky
Ached, and a stunning absence filled
Those lost and vast and cloudless spaces.

WAKING

I woke this morning wanting you; or was
It anyone, or all—her whose eyes met mine
Last night, or that sleek other one in Lahore,
Or that one lost to me ten years before
Who almost broke us, or the old decline
Into hot wandering hand and teasing tongue
Adept and flickering the soft liquid places
Merely in dreams, because such distances
Keep me from anything but dreams? When young
I would have solved it with my hand, and loathed
Myself, and thrilled with guilt, and on, and on . . .

I fell asleep again, and in sleep breathed
Your secret smell, so dear and far away.
And now I wake again, and it has gone—
That oldest hunger, unappeased—and rise
As tired men rise, simply to face the day.

CALLED FOR
Emily's

Tonight we drive back late from talk and supper
Across miles of unlit roads, flat field and fen,
Towards home; but on the way must make a detour
And rescue you from what, half-laughingly,
We think of as your temporary world—
Some group or other, all outlandishly
Named and rigged up in fancy dress and loud
With adolescent grief. Well, we're too old
For alien caperings like that. The road
Runs towards home and habit, milk and bed.

That unborn child I locked up in neat stanzas
Survives in two or three anthologies,
An effigy sealed off from chance or changes.
Now I arrive near midnight, but too early
To claim you seventeen years afterwards :
A darkened auditorium, lit fitfully
By dizzy crimsons, pulsing and fading blues
Through which electric howls and snarled-out words
Isolate you (though only in my eyes)
Sitting among three hundred sprawling bodies.

Your pale face for a second looms up through
The jerking filters, splatterings of colour
As if spawned by the music, red and blue
Over and over—there, your face again,
Not seeing me, not seeing anything,
Distinct and separate, suddenly plain
Among so many others, strangers. Smoke
Lifts as from a winter field, obscuring
All but your face, consuming, as I look,
That child I gave protective rhetoric.

Not just this place, the tribal lights, the passive
Communion of noise and being young,

47

Not just the strident music which I give
No more than half an ear to; but the sense
Of drifting out into another plane
Beyond the one I move on, and moved once
To bring you into being—that is why
I falter as I call you by your name,
Claim you, as drifting up towards me now
You smile at me, ready for us to go.